LITTLE LLAMA, LITTLE LLAMA, WHERE IS MAMA LLAMA?

Written by: Chris Roy

SHE'S NOT IN THE PEN WHERE THE PIGLETS MAKE A MESS.

www.ingramcontent.com/pod-product-compliance
Lightning Source LLC
Chambersburg PA
CBHW041715160426
43209CB00018B/1836